KING ST.

Set Two

BOOK 5

For Sale

For Sale
King Street: Readers Set Two - Book 5
Copyright © Iris Nunn 2014

Text: Iris Nunn
Editor: June Lewis
Illustrations: Pip Jones and Marta Kwasniewska

Published in 2014 by Gatehouse Media Limited

ISBN: 978-1-84231-120-2

British Library Cataloguing-in-Publication Data:
A catalogue record for this book is available from the British Library

King Street is an old street.

The houses have been there
for a long time.

Some of the people have been there
for a long time.

Now number eight
is up for sale.

They are asking a lot for it.

Sam smiled when he heard.

"They must be joking," he said.
"I could have got the whole street
for that amount in my day."

Lots of people went to look.

Everyone in the street
looked them over.

Now it has been sold.

News got around
about the new people.

"A bit posh," said Dave.

"I bet they won't shop here.
I bet they shop at the supermarket,"
said Mrs T from the corner shop.

"I hope they come to the pub," said Sid of the King's Arms.

"Let's wait and see," said Brenda.
"The new people are moving in
next week."

KING ST.

Set Two

BOOK 9

The Planning Meeting

The Planning Meeting
King Street: Readers Set Two - Book 9
Copyright © Iris Nunn 2014

Text: Iris Nunn
Editor: June Lewis
Illustrations: Pip Jones and Marta Kwasniewska

Published in 2014 by Gatehouse Media Limited

ISBN: 978-1-84231-124-0

British Library Cataloguing-in-Publication Data:
A catalogue record for this book is available from the British Library

Number two has been empty
for a year now.

They talk about pulling it down.

A supermarket wants to buy the plot
and pull the house down.

They want to buy a corner
of the park too.

A lot of people are not happy.

Mrs T is upset.

"Who will come to my shop
if there is a supermarket
down the street?"

"You could move,"
said Frank, her lodger.

"Who will buy my shop then?"

"It won't be safe for the kids
with all that traffic,"
said Gwen.

"We have too many supermarkets
in Kingsmead,"
said Mr Javindra.

So they spoke to Sid in the pub.
Sid said they could have a meeting
to talk about it.

Everyone came.

Gwen said they could all write letters to object.

Sid said they could sign a petition.

Dave said he would go
to the planning meeting
as he was not at work.

"We'll do what we can,"
he said.